Blogging
for
Beginners

Start and Maintain a Successful
Blog the Simple Way

by David Lawfield

Published in Canada

© Copyright 2015 –David Lawfield

ISBN-13: 978-1514381885
ISBN-10: 1514381885

Table of Contents

Table of Contents

Introduction

Do you have a passion for writing, and interacting with people from all over the world? If you want to become a successful blogger, you have found the perfect place to get started. Each chapter in this book is designed to walk you through an essential element of blogging. You will learn how to make a great blog, get people to visit it, and even how to make money from your hard work. You never know — you might become a blogging sensation, with quite a large income to show for it. Before all of that, the very next section will explain exactly what a blog is, in case you are not quite sure.

As with all worthwhile things, learning how to blog well takes time. Don't jump into this too quickly, or you might miss out on some important advice. Instead, take your time to read through every section of this book, and then you can go and make your blogging dreams come true.

Exactly What is a Blog

You might have a general idea of what a blog is, or perhaps you've only heard the term mentioned briefly in conversation. Either way, you're probably looking for a little more information. Luckily, you are reading just the book to give you all the information you need!

Let's start with where the term "blog" came from. It's short for "weblog", which is (you guessed it) a log that's published on the Internet.Blogs and websites often seem very similar, and that's because they are. However, a blog is more of a regularly updated online journal. They can act as a medium for self-expression, or for documented people's lives. They tend to be more personal than regular websites, and that's a big reason why they are so popular.

Blogs allow their creators to connect with readers in ways that have been traditionally frowned upon in the media. Your blog can be about anything that you want. The only real limit is your field of interests, or what your imagination allows.

Here are some more terms that will be useful to know:
Blogger: someone who creates or maintains a blog.
Blog: an Internet journal or diary.
Blog: the act of writing a blog. You can blog something, by writing about it on your blog.
Blogging (verb): the actual act of writing a blog.

Why Blog?

People blog for many reasons and much of the world agrees that it's a great activity. Here are some of the best reasons to make a blog:

It's challenging. Just the act of sitting down and writing your thoughts, so that people might want to read them, is difficult. Embrace that, because it helps you to grow as a person. Dealing with challenges is what helps people improve themselves.

You learn a lot. All of the skills that you need to master in order to blog, will improve your overall base of skills and knowledge greatly. Constantly looking for new things to blog about will also make you a more worldly person.

Reach out to people. Do you ever think that your voice isn't important? Well, it is! You'd be surprised how many people there are out there, who would love to read what you have to say to the world.

Build your business. This is one of the reasons for many people to start blogs. They are great for business, and even the largest corporations all seem to have them these days. Why don't you take advantage of the popularity of blogs for your own business?

Demonstrate your authority. You are probably an expert at something, so why not show people your authority? This is especially useful for getting the public to trust a business or brand name.

4

Chapter 1:
Types of Blogs

You might have guessed it, but there are many different types of blogs. As you venture into the wild world of blogging, it's best to be aware of the most popular types there are.

Journal Blogs

These are much like traditional diaries, where the writer shares things about their own life. Often, the goal with journals isn't to make money, since they're usually done as a hobby. However, they often do become quite successful, bringing in good money.

Business Blogs

These are one of the quickest growing types of blogs. The main goal with business blogs is to make quality content that will be useful for customers. They're used to bring in new customers, or increase loyalty.

The blogs of big companies will often have the best quality content, because they pay plenty of money to make that happen.

Niche Expert Blogs

These are typically created to bring in revenue. By making content that will be useful for a specific niche, the blogger hopes to draw high amounts of traffic. Even though their range topics is generally quite narrow, it's possible to find a huge audience with a niche expert blog.

Professional Blogs

These are a little like a mix between business and niche expert blogs. They are typically made by people who know a whole lot about their niche, and have a great passion for it. They are often made by entrepreneurs and freelancers, who are using their blogs to create more business opportunities.

The Qualities of a Successful Blogger

As you are probably aware, there are some bloggers who are just more successful than others. What makes those people different, or "better" than the rest? How have they managed to rise to the top, and make a great income from blogging in the process?

Take a look at some of the biggest qualities that the world's best bloggers typically possess:

Expertise

Yes, there are plenty of successful bloggers without special qualifications and industry jobs. However, no casual bloggers will have a good change of being successful. In order to make it in the blogging game, you need to have a huge store of knowledge about the world of blogging. A successful blogger must be an expert at blogging.

Social Butterfly

If you want to be a great blogger and you hate communicating with people, this might not be the best option for you. People who enjoy networking, and creating new connections, tend to become the best bloggers.

Influence

To learn how to make money blogging, you need to become influential. The best in the business hold a huge sway over what other people think, and could practically change the industry with their opinions and ideas. That means having a solid relationship with audiences around the world, as well as other bloggers.

Brilliant Content

No one rises to the top by sharing average content. Who do you usually seek out, when looking for advice and information? The best people in the industry, with the most outstanding content, right? You have to be able to inspire people and drive them to take action.

Offline Living

It's hard to become a successful blogger if you never leave your home. Those who rise to the top are often seen out-and-about, doing things, and taking part in special events. That includes conferences, meetings, and special gatherings.

You don't need to travel all over the world, so this part can be relatively local. However, readers love to see that their favourite bloggers are actually living a "real" life, instead of just sitting in front of a computer screen. It's all part of the human connection that people are looking for, when reading blogs.

Chapter 2:
Making Your Blog

Ingredients for a Great Blog

All good blogs share a number of things in common. While many of them vary, excelling at different aspects, below are the typical ingredients for a superb blog.

Great Media Assets

You can make a good blog that's all text, but most top bloggers use a range of different media assets to accompany their blog posts. These include things like embedded videos, quality images, and any other resources that you can think to add to your blog. This adds an extra dimension to an otherwise static-looking blog.

Personal Touch

People want to know who their favourite bloggers are. That's why it is essential to put a face to the content — and that should be *your* face. The big corporations often have faceless, nameless content. This is where you can get an advantage, by making sure to put a face behind your blog.

Social Media Tools

If you want people to share your content on social media, you had better make it easy for them. There are loads of tool that you can use to help people with social sharing, like ShareThis and AddThis.

Conversations

One of the reasons that blogs are so popular is that visitors are largely encouraged to join in on conversations. Make sure that people are able to easily leave comments, and interact with not only you, but other commenter's. Try to encourage people to start discussions, and you will find that your popularity grows.

Regular Content Uploads

Are you planning to publish 10 posts soon? Instead of putting them online all in one day, why not spread them out over a week or so? It's much better to have just one or two posts every day, instead of leaving a big gap in between batches of uploads.

Analyze Your Data

If you want to make the best decisions about your blog, it's important to use analytical tools. How many people are visiting your blog every day? What did they look at, and how long were they on the page? You can use Google Analytics for free, and it will tell you everything that you'll need to know. Another popular option is Webtrends.

Chapter 3:
WordPress.org VS
WordPress.com

If you have decided to use WordPress to create your blog, as many people do, you might be wondering where to start. The first question that a lot of beginners have is, "What's the difference between WordPress.org and WordPress.com?" It's a valid question, and the two are quite different. To give a quick answer, you should definitely choose WordPress.org for any serious blog.

WordPress.org

To use this version of WordPress, you will need to have your own web host, and that will cost you a little money. After this, you can do what you like with it (within the law), and monetize as you see fit. WordPress will not put their own ads on your site either, which is a big plus.

This is the more difficult option, but it's honestly the only way to go for anyone who wants to blog professionally on WordPress.

WordPress.com

This is a completely free option, where you can sign up to make your own website or blog very quickly. However, there are some limitations about what you can do with your site. You will not need to worry about setting anything up manually, however.

In order to get rid of limitations, like using customized plugins or removing advertisements, you will need to pay. It also doesn't allow you to use ads from other sources, like Google AdSense. That is why it's not the best option for making a professional blog.

Chapter 4:
Writing Golden Content for Your Blog

If there is one thing that you should remember from this book, it's that *Content Is King*. Why do people visit blogs and websites? They're looking for brilliant content. They want something that will help them in their lives, inspire them, provide them with useful information, or give great value in some other way.

People are not looking for some spam-ridden advertising on a blog post. If you think that you can just upload a bunch of filler, think again. There is already *way* too much junk on the Internet. Anyone who is dedicated to becoming a number one blogger needs to hone their skills at making supreme content. If you can't do it yourself, you need to hire other people who can.

Headlines Are Important

This is the first thing that people see, and they won't usually bother investigating content that has a bad headline. Often, people will share or like something purely based on a good headline, even if they don't read the rest of the post. You need to get into the habit of making killer headlines for your content.

You can make a headline that promotes a sense of urgency in people, one that tells others why your post will be useful, something that seems very unique, or just make one that's highly specific. People generally don't like vague headlines, like "The Best Post Ever".

Learn from Others

You don't need to reinvent the wheel here. Seriously, anything that you can possibly think of has already been done in some way. It might be a little different, with varying angles, etc., but you don't have to worry about making something *completely* different.

Having said that, you *can* make present your content in new ways, so don't give up on being creative just yet.

Learn to Write Well

Make sure that you write content that has a "wow" factor, so people don't get bored. Look through your writing, and figure out if you tend to overuse certain words of phrases. Keep your writing interesting, and easy-to-read, so people aren't turned away from your content.

It also helps to learn the basics of grammar and composition, so that your blog looks somewhat professional. There's a fine line between being quirky, and looking like you don't know how to write.

Give Surprises

Inspire some sort of emotion in people, whether they're happy, mad, sad, or even irritated. Some people go for the shock factor with their blog posts, while others try to create something that will get people thinking, and talking.

Show, Don't Tell

This is an old piece of writing advice, but it's still highly relevant. If you want people to take you seriously, don't just *tell* them about something — show them why they should trust you. If you say that lots of people are spending too much time on their smart phones, make sure that you back it up with trustworthy sources. Don't be afraid to link to other sites, to give people some further reading to do. Providing quotes is another good way to state your sources.

Chapter 5:
Traffic and Advertising

Advertising on Your Blog

There are loads of ways to add advertisements to a blog. Selecting the right options for you might take some experimentation. The most popular advertising services are Yahoo Publisher and Google Adsense, but those are just two of the many choices you have. Many people use just one of these services, and have a lot of success. It's recommended that you stick with Adsense for now, and possibly use some affiliate marketing (discussed in the next chapter).

Google Adsense

This service lets you place many different types of ads on your blog. They are "contextual", meaning they change, depending on your content.

That means that people are more likely to click on the ads, bringing you more money. You won't need to concern yourself with choosing different ads, so this is a great way to boost your income.

All you need to do is sign up with Google Adsense. Once you have done that, you need to create ad campaigns, and then use the special codes with your blog. They will need some information from you, including a method for payment, and verification of who you are.

Yahoo Publisher

This words similarly to Adsense, but they will only allow high traffic websites to use their service. That means this is not a great option for people who are just starting out. However, the share of revenue for their publishers (that's you) is generally higher.

Drive Traffic to Your Blog

Many people have gone through this scenario: they create a blog, publish some content, and then sit around waiting for people to start visiting. If that's the approach that you hope to take — forget it. Unless you are somehow very lucky, or your posts suddenly become viral, it's just not going to happen.

If you want to create a successful blog, you are going to need visitors — lots and lots of them. To increase the number of people who visit your site everyday, take a look at the following tips.

Share Multiple Times

A lot of bloggers do not share their content nearly enough. You can't just expect to publish, share on a single social site or forum, and wait for the traffic to come charging in. You should be sharing every post as many times as possible. That means you will want to use things like Facebook, Twitter, Google+, Reddit, StumbleUpon, Instagram, etc. There are plenty of places for people to share links and content, so why not take advantage of them all?

You are probably thinking that this could quickly start to take up too much time. Instead of manually going through, and sharing your content on each platform, use some automation. There are a lot of great plugins and services for sharing content. Take some time to do some searching, and find something that does what *you* need.

Hire Influential Bloggers

If you want to rise to the top quickly, try utilizing the popularity of other writers. Find people who already have a large audience, and lots of respect in their niche. Ask them if they will write for you, and be sure to specify that you want them to share your blog's content on their own platforms.

Unless you already have a popular blog, it's unlikely that you'll get any successful bloggers on your team. If that's the case, you will probably have to pay them. However, the boost that it could give your blog is well worth paying for.

This is often a better approach than just hiring a freelance writer, who doesn't have much of an audience.

You can always ask other bloggers if they would be willing to trade posts with you. Maybe you could write something for them, and they would in turn return the favour. Each of you would benefit from the increased exposure for your blogs, and yourselves. This approach will only work if you are a relatively popular blogger already.

Perfect Your Social Posts

You already know that sharing your content on social media is important. But *how* you do so is equally important. Of course, sharing a link to the relevant content is necessary, but what else would you write? Something like "Check this out" is not going to work very well. It's too vague, so most people will tend to scroll past it. Instead, how about writing the title of your post? You should have spent time to come up with a great one, so use it. That way, people will quickly see the title, and it will work to draw them in. They will hopefully click on your link, and go to your blog post.

SEO

Search engine optimization is one of the most important aspects of getting website traffic. If you want search engines, like Google, to send people to your content — you need to play by their rules. SEO is a complex topic, especially if you're new to this whole blogging thing. There are loads of resources out there, so you should have no trouble learning proper SEO. However, this is a book about blogging, so it won't be discussed in detail here.

Chapter 6:
Advertising Networks

One of the main ways to make money with a blog is through advertising. Companies are willing to pay big dollars to anyone willing to display ads to lots of visitors.

If you want to use something other than Adsense or Yahoo Publisher, you have a lot of choices for advertisers. There are many networks that will make the task easier, so you don't need to go and find willing advertisers on your own.

Here are some of the biggest advertising networks out there, that have not already been mentioned in this chapter:

BlogAds

You need to have a niche blog that gets at least 30,000 hits per month, in order to use this network. If you have a broader theme to your blog, you will need a minimum of 500,000, up to one million, hits per month.

Federated Media

This company started out as a marketing and digital media company, located in San Fransisco. Since then, they have expanded their business, and place advertising through popular blogs.

Chitika

This company claims to display four million ads every month, over at least 200,000 different sites.

Google AdSense

This was mentioned earlier in the chapter, but it's worth noting AdSense again. Be sure to look into this network, even if you only use one.

Email Marketing

Many people think of email marketing as sort of outdated. It's understandable, because email has been around just about as long as the Internet. However, that's no reason to overlook this extremely useful marketing tool. If you are not using emails as part of your marketing strategy — you are going to miss out on traffic, and income.

To get started with email marketing, you are going to need to build your list. There are plugins that you can use on your blog, that will allow people to sign up to your email newsletter or mailing list. Be sure to get people's permission, before you start sending them anything. That means you can't simply start compiling emails from random people on the Internet.

Once you have a list of visitors, you can begin your email campaign. Using a service, like MailChimp or Aweber, is the easiest way to do so. They have easy-to-use tools for compiling your list, and sending out regular emails. Better still, you can use their services to see how effective your emails are at reaching out to your users.

Selling Ads Directly

If you'd rather take advertisement into your own hands, it's possible to sell ad space on your blog directly. That will make sure that all the profits go to you, and allow you to do things however you like.

First, you will need to find some prospective advertisers. Companies that sell goods or services related to your blog are a good start. Next, contact them and ask if they would like to advertise with you.

Before you start emailing every company on the web, put together a list of the types and sizes of ads you would like to offer. You're also going to need a price list, so people know what kind of value they can get. No one is going to want to advertise with you, unless you have some statistics to demonstrate that your blog is actually popular.

You will need a method for payment, too, since you're doing this on your own. <u>Paypal</u> is a very popular way to get paid online, and it's free to make an account.

Should You Use Popup Ads?

The dreaded popup has earned a place in people's memories, and it's not positive. Because of pushy advertisers, trying to force users to look at their ads, a lot of people *hate* popups. Does that mean that you shouldn't use them? Not necessarily. While no one wants to be interrupted while they're trying to surf the web, you can still use popups in a more careful way.

A great use of popup ads is to collect email signups from your users. Since you're not trying to sell people anything, they should be happy to see a small opt-in window popup somewhere on their screen. This is probably the only reason that you should use these types of ads on your blog, because as mentioned, people don't much like them in any other form.

Should You Use Pop-up Ads?

Chapter 7:
Making Money

Monetizing Your New Blog

When you're just starting out, it might be tempting to load your blog with ads right away. Since you probably won't have much traffic, this method isn't going to earn you much — if any — money. But that doesn't mean you shouldn't use the ads right away. Just make sure that they're not absolutely plastered all over your blog, or people might assume that you're only in it for the money. As mentioned already — visitors want someone they can like, instead of a shallow salesperson.

If you plan to sell things directly, it's a good idea to put them up for display on your blog right away. That's how a physical store would do things, right? It's a good idea to get into the habit of monetizing your blog when you first begin.

Sell Your Blog

You are probably aware that people buy real estate properties, possibly fix them up, and then sell them for big bucks. You can do the same thing with a blog or website. The best part is that a blog costs *very* little to create. Apart from web hosting, a domain name, and any other things you might choose to buy, it doesn't really cost anything. That means that just about anyone can earn money by starting blogs, making them successful, and then selling them to the highest bidder.

There are web services that allow you to sell your blog to buyers. Some good sites for this are SitePoint Auctions, NamePros, Flippa, and Businesses For Sale.

Affiliate Marketing Basics

Have you ever seen an interesting blog post, or product review, that had links to a product? The chances are, if you were to click that link and choose to buy the product, the blogger who sent you there would get some money. That's basically what affiliate marketing is about.

If you have a lot of users who trust your opinions, you can recommend products to them. There's nothing dishonest here either, because most people tell their readers that they're looking at ad links.

The primary affiliate link service at the moment is with Amazon. You can write helpful information about different products, and then include affiliate links to them. Don't think of it as trying to sell things. The chances are that your readers are interested in the things that you buy anyway.

Rather than making just a small amount when visitors click on regular ads, you can make some large percentages with affiliate advertisements. If you successfully link to an expensive item, you could start to see a *huge* increase in your monthly income from your blog.

You don't need to limit yourself to physical products either. There are lots of digital products, like eBooks, interactive courses, audio, and video, to affiliate yourself with. The best part about electronic formats, is that the profit margin is often quite high for the creators. They don't need to make a physical item, so they might be willing to share a higher percentage with you.

Paid Posts and Sponsored Reviews

Just like celebrities and athletes are paid to endorse companies, bloggers can also earn money in this fashion. There are a lot of people willing to pay money, to have popular bloggers endorse their goods and services. If you have a lot of fans, why not make the most of it, and earn some extra cash in return? Perhaps you can organize some sort of competition through your sponsors, so that your visitors can have the chance to win some great prizes.

Here are some good sponsoring networks to look into: SponsoredReviews, PayPerPost, ReviewMe, SocialSpark, and PayU2Blog.

Selling Products and Services

Many people use blogs as an accompaniment to a webstore or online business. You can get a lot of people to visit your site with a blog, so this is a wonderful technique. People will go to your blog for the great content, and then you can encourage them to buy whatever you are selling.

This type of approach tends to work well, compared to a more general online store. The use of a blog makes you more approachable, and creating great content will show people that you know your stuff. Would you rather buy something from a generic-looking store, or from a person who is an authority in their industry?

Audio Advertising

A lot of the content online is in the form of text, images, and videos too these days. You might think that audio went out of fashion when radio was replaced by television, as the dominant media. Advertisements in audio form are starting to become more popular, however. With the rise of podcasts, and more people using the Internet to stream audio, it makes sense to think about audio ads again.

There are lots of companies willing to pay you, in order to have their audio ads placed on your site. Don't overlook this valuable platform, because it could make you a ton of money.

Find Paid Blogging Jobs

If you'd rather get paid to blog, without going through the trouble of creating your own blog, there are some great options to choose from. Top writers can earn some good money by selling their content directly to blogs. While you can get upfront payments by doing this, some networks will give you a share of their advertising revenue, from your blog posts. That's a big incentive to write the best posts possible, even though they won't be used for your own blog.

Some popular places to find paid blogging gigs include: Freelance Writing Jobs, ProBlogger.net, Elance, Freelance Switch, and Performancing.

Conclusion

Are you still interested in becoming a successful blogger? Hopefully you are now more motivated that ever to get out there, and start blogging like crazy! The information that you've learned from this book will help you on the way to becoming one of the greats. Of course, you can't expect it to be easy. Anyone who says you can become an overnight success — is lying, and probably trying to sell you some useless product to make it possible. The only way to see success as a blogger is to stick to the fundamentals discussed in this book, and keep on learning new methods on top of those.

The first thing you need to do is decide what you'd like to blog about. Once you have a good idea, set up some web hosting, get yourself a platform (like WordPress) — and begin uploading at least one post *every day*. Good luck, future blogger!

DISCLAIMER AND/OR LEGAL NOTICES: Every effort has been made to accurately represent this book and it's potential. Results vary with every individual, and your results may or may not be different from those depicted. No promises, guarantees or warranties, whether stated or implied, have been made that you will produce any specific result from this book. Your efforts are individual and unique, and may vary from those shown. Your success depends on your efforts, background and motivation.

The material in this publication is provided for educational and informational purposes only and is not intended as medical advice. The information contained in this book should not be used to diagnose or treat any illness, metabolic disorder, disease or health problem. Always consult your physician or health care provider before beginning any nutrition or exercise program. Use of the programs, advice, and information contained in this book is at the sole choice and risk of the reader.